12 ETUDES FOR CLAR

by

Victor Polatschek

**First Clarinetist with the
Boston Symphony Orchestra**

These twelve etudes are designed to develop an even and precise finger technique. The staccato exercises, Nos. 4 and 5, will help the student achieve perfect synchronization of fingers and tongue.

Some of these studies are based on motives of well known pieces, as for example No. 1, on the motive of the last movement of the C major Piano Sonata by Weber (the so-called *Perpetuum Mobile*), and No. 3, on that of the Prelude to the fourth act of *Carmen*.

ISBN 978-0-7935-5271-9

EDWARD B.
Marks Music
COMPANY

EXCLUSIVELY DISTRIBUTED BY
HAL•LEONARD®
CORPORATION
7777 W. BLUEMOUND RD. P.O. BOX 13819 MILWAUKEE, WI 53213

M 416

12 Etudes for Clarinet

VIVACE

Victor Polatschek

ALLEGRO

2.

3. ALLEGRO VIVACE

ANDANTE MOSSO

4.

ALLEGRO MODERATO

ANDANTE MOSSO

6.

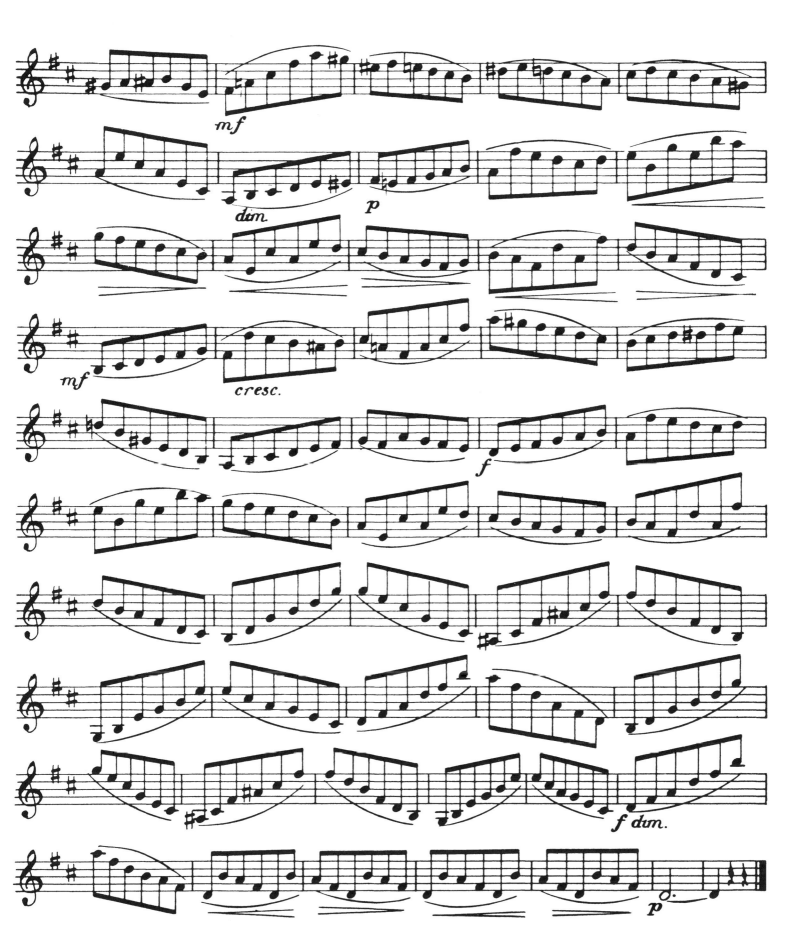

ALLEGRO

7.

cresc.

f

ff

ANDANTE MOSSO

8.

18

ANDANTINO

10.

12527-23

VIVACE

11.

MODERATO